McGraw-Hill Reading Wonders

CCSS Reading/Language Arts Program

Program Authors

Diane August	Jan Hasbrouck
Donald R. Bear	Margaret Kilgo
Janice A. Dole	Jay McTighe
Jana Echevarria	Scott G. Paris
Douglas Fisher	Timothy Shanahan
David Francis	Josefina V. Tinajero
Vicki Gibson	

McGraw Hill Education

Bothell, WA • Chicago, IL • Columbus, OH • New York, NY

Cover and Title Pages: Nathan Love

www.mheonline.com/readingwonders C

The *McGraw·Hill* Companies

Education

Copyright © 2014 by The McGraw-Hill Companies, Inc.

Send all inquiries to:
McGraw-Hill Education
Two Penn Plaza
New York, NY 10121

ISBN: 978-0-02-119716-3
MHID: 0-02-119716-4

Printed in the United States of America.

5 6 7 8 9 RMN 17 16 15 14

Unit 5 Wonders of Nature

The Big Idea: What kinds of things can you find growing in nature?

Watch It Grow!

Talk About It

How can you care for a garden?

Hh

Say the name of each picture.

Read each word.

3 **hop**   **ham**   **hip**

4 **hot**   **hid**   **him**

my

Do you like **my** hat?

It is hot in **my** garden.

7

Hop Can Hop!

8

I am Dot.
I like Hop.

I am hot.
See **my** hat on top!

Hop is hot.
Hop can hop on top.

Jan Bryan-Hunt

11

Hop can hop, hop, hop.

I can hop, hop, hop!

I can sit.
Hop can sit.

Pop and I can sip.
Hop can sip.

Organization

Look at the poem that Jamal wrote. The poem tells about a flower Jamal likes.

Jamal's Model

It is sweet.

It is blue.

Can you smell it?

I can, too!

George Hamblin

Pronouns

A pronoun is a word that is used in place of a noun.

She set the cup on the table.

He waters the flowers.

Essential Question
How do living things change as they grow?

Go Digital!

Growing Tall

Talk About It

How will this tree change?

Ee

Say the name of each picture.

Read each word.

| 3 | **Ed** | **pet** | **ten** |
| 4 | **den** | **net** | **met** |

are

Ted and Ed **are** friends.

The branches **are** bare.

Ed and Ned

Ed is not a pet.
Ned is not a pet.

Ned is up, up, up.
See Ned! See Ned!

Ed met Ned.
Ned met Ed.

Ed can sip, sip, sip.
Ned can sip, sip, sip.

Are Ed and Ned hot?
Are Ed and Ned wet?

27

Ed can hop, hop, hop.

Ned can nap, nap, nap.

Organization

Read Tara's sentences. Tara tells about
a book she read.

Tara's model

I liked <u>Trees Grow.</u>
My favorite tree
was the tree
in fall.

George Hamblin

Pronouns

A pronoun is a word that is used in place of a noun.

You and I can plant the tree.

We both like roses!

Gary Lacoste

31

Essential Question

What kinds of things grow on a farm?

Go Digital!

Farm Fresh

Talk About It

What food do you see?

33

Say the name of each picture.

Read each word.

3 **fin**   **fed**   **fan**

4 **rip**   **rat**   **rod**

he	with

He picked a red apple.

I go **with** Ron to the farm.

35

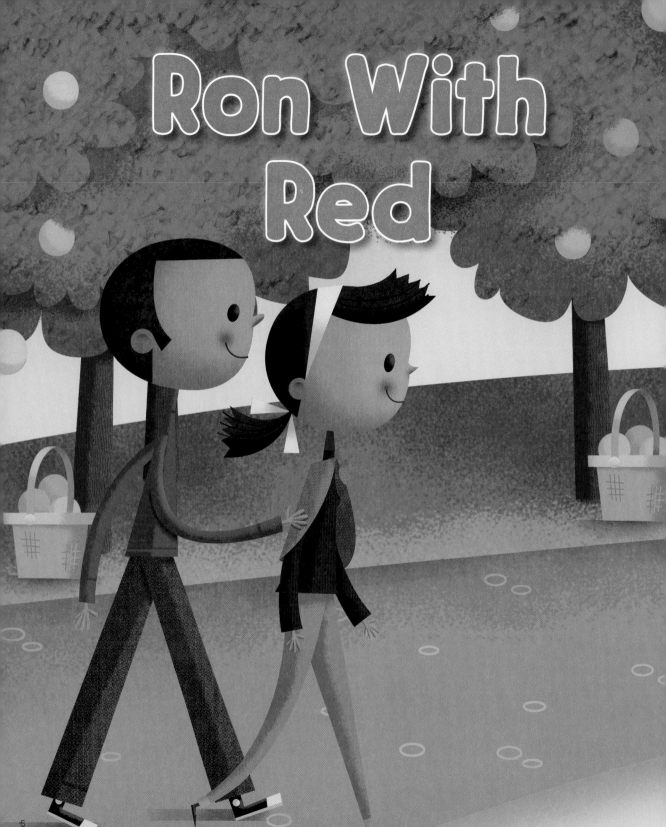

Ron With Red

Ron is **with** Red.

Red is a pet.

Chris Lensch

Chris Lensch

Red can see a  bird.

Can Ron see it on top?

Dad can see ten  .

oranges

He can fit ten in a  .

basket

39

Red can see a  bird.

Can Ron see it on top?

Mom can see ten .
tomatoes

Mom can fit ten on top.

Ron can sit and sip.

Red can see a .

bird

Ron did not see a .
bird

Red can see it on top!

Organization

Read Trevor's story. Trevor tells a story about apples.

Trevor's Model

Mom and I go to an apple farm. We pick apples. They taste sweet!

Pronouns

A pronoun is a word that is used in place of a noun.

We pick blueberries.

He grows red cherries.

Gary Lacoste